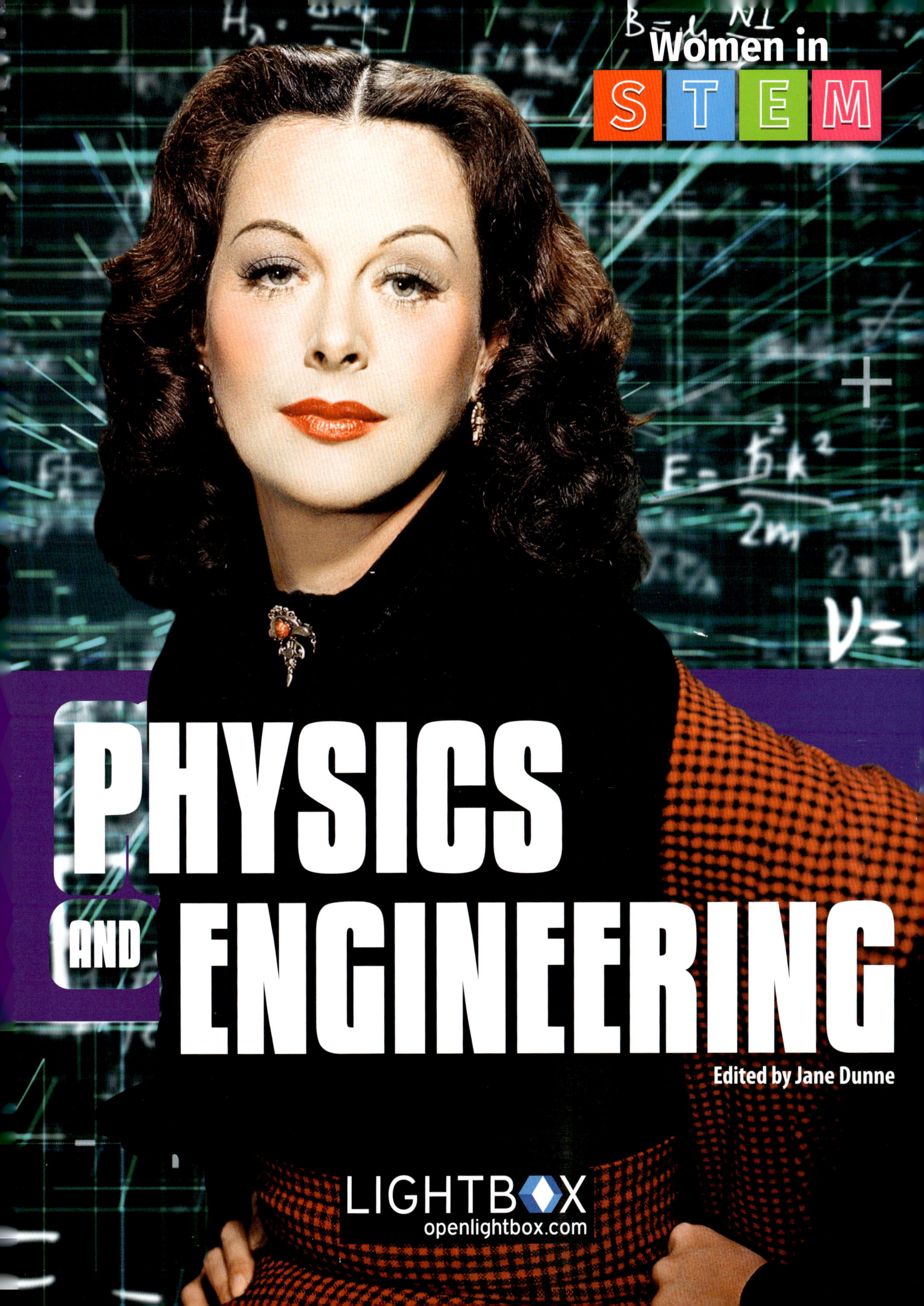
Women in
STEM
PHYSICS
AND ENGINEERING
Edited by Jane Dunne
LIGHTBOX
openlightbox.com

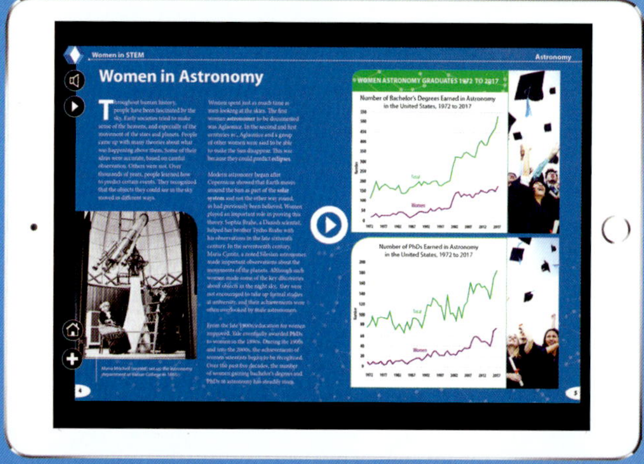

Lightbox is an all-inclusive digital solution for the teaching and learning of curriculum topics in an original, groundbreaking way. Lightbox is based on National Curriculum Standards.

STANDARD FEATURES OF LIGHTBOX

AUDIO High-quality narration using text-to-speech system

ACTIVITIES Printable PDFs that can be emailed and graded

SLIDESHOWS Pictorial overviews of key concepts

VIDEOS Embedded high-definition video clips

WEBLINKS Curated links to external, child-safe resources

TRANSPARENCIES Step-by-step layering of maps, diagrams, charts, and timelines

INTERACTIVE MAPS Interactive maps and aerial satellite imagery

QUIZZES Ten multiple choice questions that are automatically graded and emailed for teacher assessment

KEY WORDS Matching key concepts to their definitions

PHYSICS AND ENGINEERING

CONTENTS

Women in Physics

The ancient Greek **philosopher**, Aristotle, was the first person to use the term "physics" when he wrote about motion, **gravity**, and the planets in the fourth century BC. Physics is the study of **matter** and energy, and how they behave. Perhaps the most important discovery in physics was Isaac Newton's theory of gravity in the 1600s. Newton was a mathematician, physicist, and astronomer. He realized that the force of gravity made smaller objects move toward larger ones.

In the centuries following Newton's discoveries, many women physicists played an important part in the science. Laura Bassi was an Italian scientist in the 1700s. She was the first woman to became a physics professor at a European university, although as a woman she was not allowed to give lectures to the students. However, she greatly influenced students at the University of Bologna. In 1751, a 19-year-old woman was awarded a PhD in physics.

In the 1800s, some women in Europe, such as Scotland's Mary Somerville, did research in physics. However, the first PhD in physics in the United States was not awarded until 1897. The University of Chicago awarded it to Isabelle Stone for her work on electrical resistance.

Women physicists played an important role in the development of nuclear power. Their efforts contributed to the making of the powerful atomic bombs that ended World War II.

In 1900, 836 scientists attended the first International Congress of Physics in Paris. Isabelle Stone and the chemist and physicist Marie Curie were the only women. By the middle of the 1900s, however, women were playing a leading role. Lise Meitner and Maria Goeppert Mayer made important advances in the study of **atoms**. Women scientists have also been vital in the practical applications of physics—such as communications, construction, and electrical engineering.

Today, physicists continue in their search to uncover the secrets of the universe. However, since the end of the twentieth century, the percentage of women gaining PhDs in physics has barely increased, and the numbers of women gaining degrees in physics have fallen.

Investigating how light works is a core subject in physics. In 2018, Donna Strickland won a Nobel Prize for her work in this area.

ADVANCED DEGREES IN PHYSICS IN THE UNITED STATES 2006–2016

Master's Degree	2006	2007	2008	2009	2010	2011	2012	2013	2014	2015	2016
Physics all students	1,853	1,792	1,799	1,657	1,810	1,771	1,879	1,984	1,876	1,934	1,959
Physics women	439	417	378	371	410	404	409	401	439	436	433

In 2006, 23.7 percent of all students gaining a degree in physics were female. This percentage fell to 22.1 in 2016.

PhD	2006	2007	2008	2009	2010	2010	2012	2013	2014	2015	2016
Physics all students	1,341	1,442	1,507	1,580	1,570	1,670	1,752	1,740	1,768	1,840	1,833
Physics women	234	265	280	293	305	302	350	335	331	367	354

In 2006, 17.4 percent of all students gaining a PhD in physics were female. This percentage rose to 19.3 in 2016.

Physics Worldwide

From ancient times, people all over the world have been fascinated by the universe. The science of physics was driven by a curiosity about the world, and a desire to understand how it works. The science of light is called optics. It aims to answer the mystery of what makes light. During **The Age of Enlightenment** in Europe in the 1700s, women physicists helped to spread Isaac Newton's theories about optics and the force of gravity. In the early 1800s, women physicists in Great Britain carried out experiments using magnetism and electricity. In China, scientists used Newton's principles to develop experiments using light-reflecting telescopes.

By the 1900s, universities across the globe began to offer places to women physicists. However, educational opportunities for women scientists at the high-school level were restricted until World War II ended in 1945. By the end of the century, women were playing a crucial role in the development and study of physics and engineering worldwide.

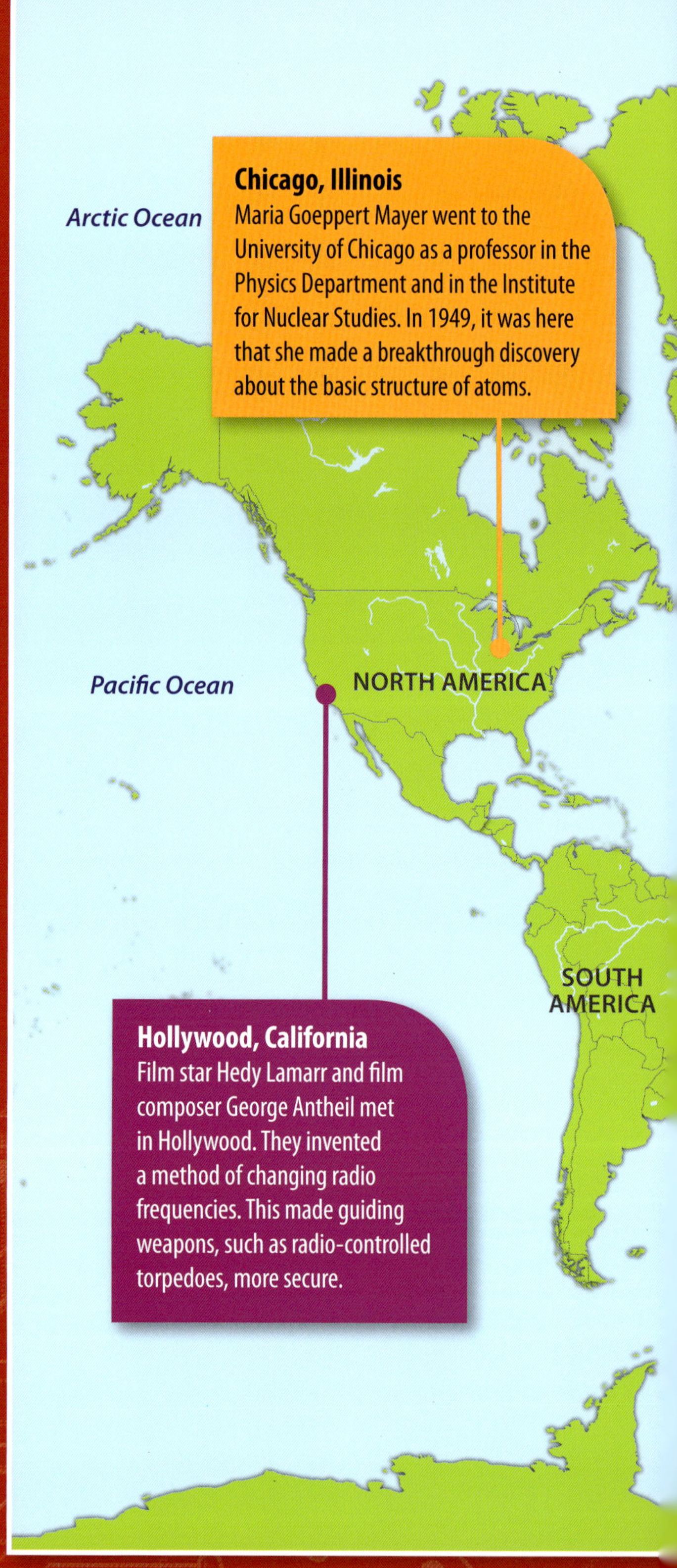

Chicago, Illinois
Maria Goeppert Mayer went to the University of Chicago as a professor in the Physics Department and in the Institute for Nuclear Studies. In 1949, it was here that she made a breakthrough discovery about the basic structure of atoms.

Hollywood, California
Film star Hedy Lamarr and film composer George Antheil met in Hollywood. They invented a method of changing radio frequencies. This made guiding weapons, such as radio-controlled torpedoes, more secure.

Arctic Ocean
London, Great Britain
Hertha Ayrton solved the problem of why the electric lights on London's streets hissed. She worked out that it was caused by a chemical reaction with oxygen in the air.
Beijing, China
Huang Lü was the first woman in China to experiment with light and magnification. She invented a telescope that could take simple photographs using light-sensitive paper.
EUROPE
Atlantic Ocean
ASIA
Pacific Ocean
Indian Ocean
AFRICA
Berlin, Germany
Lise Meitner worked in Berlin in the 1920s and 1930s. Her work involved experiments with atoms. In 1939, she realized that atoms could be broken up to release enormous amounts of energy. This led to the development of the **atomic bomb**.
AUSTRALIA
MAP LEGEND
Land
Water
N
SCALE
0
1,000 miles
1,000 kilometers
Southern Ocean
ANTARCTICA

Hertha Ayrton

Name: Hertha Ayrton
Born: 1854, Portsmouth, Great Britain
Died: 1923 Bexhill, Great Britain
Occupation: Physicist and inventor
Education: Cambridge University, and University of London
Major discoveries and achievements: Twenty-six new inventions, including the "Ayrton Fan," discovered why electric streetlights made a hissing sound
Major honors: Hughes Medal, an annual prize for physics awarded by the British Royal Society, 1906

Hertha Ayrton's parents were Polish immigrants to Great Britain. Hertha's father was a watchmaker and her mother was a seamstress. They worked hard to earn enough money for their family of eight children. At age 9, Hertha went to a school in London run by her aunt. After leaving school at age 16, Hertha started working as a governess.

Hertha had to struggle to have her work widely recognized. She became active in women's rights and the movement for women to be given the right to vote.

One of Hertha's employers was a wealthy woman called Barbara Bodichon. She was a supporter of women's education and paid for Hertha to go to Girton College, Cambridge. Girton College was the first all-women's university in England. There, Hertha studied math, and started to invent things. Her first invention measured blood pressure. In 1884, she **patented** a "line divider," which could be used to mark out a line into equal parts. This was useful for engineers. The same year, Hertha attended evening classes on electricity. Her tutor was William Ayrton, a pioneer of electrical engineering. Hertha and William married, and she helped with his experiments.

Electric arc lights were used for street lighting and stage effects in the late 1800s. Hertha improved the technology, making lighting brighter and less noisy.

Hertha also published her own work. In the 1880s, electric streetlights tended to hiss and splutter. While she was experimenting, she made a scientific breakthrough. She found that the hissing sound was due to a chemical reaction called **oxidation**. This discovery led to international recognition for Hertha.

In Great Britain, she was refused membership of the Royal Society. This was the world's oldest scientific academy, and it did not admit women. However, in 1906, the Society awarded her the Hughes Medal for her work on the ripple effects of water on sand. Later inventions included the "Ayrton Fan," which helped to lessen the effects of poison gas in the trenches during World War I.

IMPORTANT PHYSICISTS BEFORE HERTHA AYRTON

Democtritus was a Greek philosopher who lived in the fifth century BC. He is credited with being the first person to propose the theory that all matter must consist of tiny particles, which he called atoms.

Isaac Newton's work was the start of modern physics. He worked on light and optics, and also recognized the importance of the force of gravity to control motion.

Alessandro Volta was an Italian scientist. He invented a battery that could produce electricity. This made it easier for scientists to experiment with using electricity.

Michael Faraday was an English physicist. He worked out how to create and control **electromagnetism** in the early 1800s.

Working in the mid-1800s, James Clerk Maxwell demonstrated that electricity, light, and magnetism were all part of the same set of forces. He came up with a formula that linked all the scientific theories of the time.

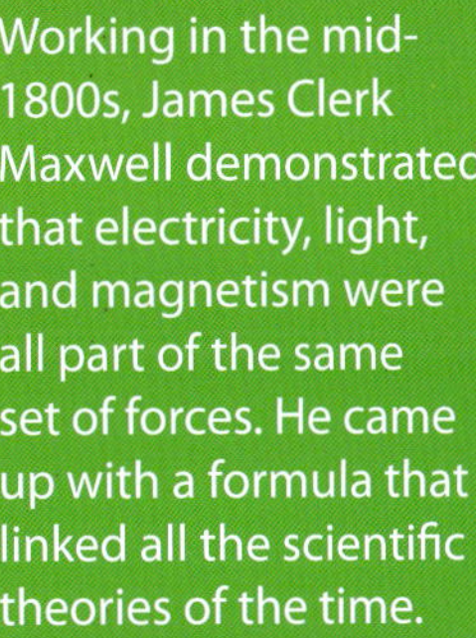

Lise Meitner

Name: Lise Meitner
Born: 1878, Vienna, Austria
Died: 1968, Cambridge, Great Britain
Occupation: Physicist
Education: University of Vienna
Major discoveries and achievements: Publishing the theory of the power of **nuclear fission**
Major honors: The civilian class of the *Pour le Mérite*, Germany's highest honor, in 1957. Element 109 was named "meitnerium" for her.

Lise Meitner's parents were wealthy and encouraged her interest in science. They supported her financially when she left home to study physics at the University of Vienna.

She was only the second woman to be awarded a PhD in physics by the university. In 1907, Lise moved to the University of Berlin in Germany. At the university, she met radiochemist Otto Hahn. They began a 30-year working partnership. However, as a female scientist, she was not allowed to have a paid job at the university, so she worked as an unpaid researcher. Working alongside Hahn and another scientist, Fritz Strassman, Lise's work involved seeing whether they could artificially create a new substance. They tried bombarding uranium atoms with neutrons.

In 1938, Lise was forced to flee Berlin. She was Jewish. The Nazi Party that ruled Germany was putting Jews in prison.

Lise Meitner spent much of her life working in Sweden and Great Britain. She refused to work on atomic or nuclear weapons.

b) to speed up the experimental work, which is at present being carried on within the limits of the budgets of University laboratories, by providing funds, if such funds be required, through his contacts with private persons who are willing to make contributions for this cause, and perhaps also by obtaining the co-operation of industrial laboratories which have the necessary equipment.

I understand that Germany has actually stopped the sale of uranium from the Czechoslovakian mines which she has taken over. That she should have taken such early action might perhaps be understood on the ground that the son of the German Under-Secretary of State, von Weizsäcker, is attached to the Kaiser-Wilhelm-Institut in Berlin where some of the American work on uranium is now being repeated.

Yours very truly,
A. Einstein
(Albert Einstein)

Albert Einstein wrote to the president of the United States. He suggested the United States work to create an atomic bomb before Germany could make such a weapon.

Meitner fled to Sweden, but continued to keep in touch with Hahn by letter. They continued their experiments with uranium, but the results were surprising. They had expected the uranium atoms would become heavier, but instead they became lighter.

In January 1939, Meitner realized what was happening. It was a process that had not been recognized before. It was nuclear fission. Enormous amounts of energy were released as the **nucleus** of the uranium atom was bombarded. Albert Einstein, another great scientist, wrote to President Franklin D. Roosevelt that Lise's discovery meant a very powerful bomb could be built. The United States set up a program to develop nuclear fission. The first atomic bomb was dropped in 1945.

The energy in **nuclear fuel** is more than

10 MILLION TIMES more powerful than that contained in gasoline.

The **atomic bomb** dropped on the Japanese city of Hiroshima in 1945 is estimated to have killed between **90,000 and 166,000** people.

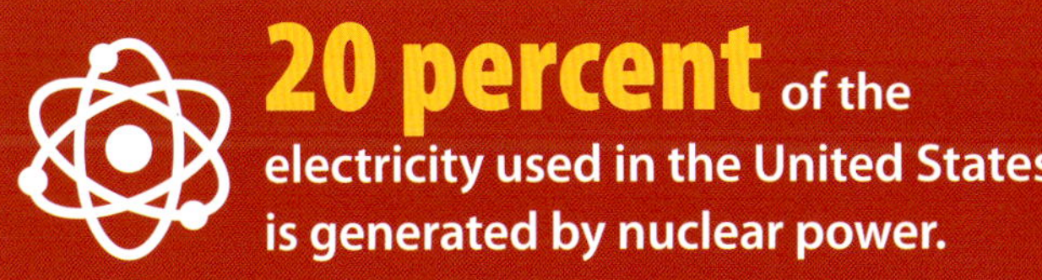

Maria Goeppert Mayer

Name: Maria Goeppert Mayer
Born: 1906, Kattowitz, Germany
Died: 1972, San Diego, California
Occupation: Physicist
Education: University of Gottingen
Major discoveries and achievements: Creating a model of how atoms are constructed
Major honors: Elected a Fellow of the American Academy of Arts and Sciences in 1965, winner of the Nobel Prize in Physics, 1963

Maria Goeppert was born in Kattowitz, Germany, which is now Katowice, in Poland. Her father was a university professor, and Maria was encouraged in her scientific studies. She went to a school that welcomed female science students. When Maria went to study math at the University of Göttingen, her math professor was the star mathematician Emmy Noether. Although outstanding at math, Maria decided she wanted to be a physicist. Her later PhD thesis was described as a "masterpiece."

Maria found that being married made it difficult for her career in the 1930s. Married women were discouraged from working.

Maria married physicist Joseph Edward Mayer in 1930 and they moved to the United States. He became a professor at Johns Hopkins University, but wives were not allowed to become professors. For a time, she worked unpaid, but, in 1943, she was asked to join the U.S. government Manhattan Project. The project was doing research into atomic weapons. Maria's work was with a team taking natural uranium and separating it to make weapons-quality uranium that could be used in atomic bombs.

After World War II, Maria took up a post at the University of Chicago. When she took the job, she claimed that she knew nothing about nuclear physics. However, in 1949, she came up with a model for the structure of atoms and the way the protons and neutrons behave. Protons and neutrons are the small particles at the centre of an atom. Maria described how the protons and neutrons are arranged in rings or shells, like the layers of an onion. This breakthrough is called the nuclear shell model. It took her another few years to work out the practical consequences of such a discovery.

In her PhD thesis in 1930, Maria had put forward theories about packets of light, or photons. In 1961, these theories were proven to be correct by experiments made with a new invention, the laser.

While Maria was researching the shell model, three other German scientists were also working on the problem. They all shared the Nobel Prize in Physics in 1963.

There are about **7 billion billion billion** atoms in the **human body.**

A typical drop of water contains **2 sextillion** oxygen atoms and **4 sextillion** hydrogen atoms. A sextillion has 21 zeroes!

Atoms are tiny. A **single human hair** is about **1 MILLION** carbon atoms in width.

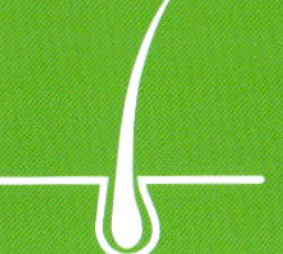

WALTZING TOWARD NUCLEAR STRUCTURE

Maria described how she came upon the idea of the nuclear shell. She thought in terms of dancing. "Think of a room full of waltzers. Suppose they go round the room in circles, each circle enclosed within another. Then imagine that in each circle, you can fit twice as many dancers by having one pair go clockwise and another pair go counterclockwise. Then add one more variation; all the dancers are spinning twirling round and round like tops as they circle the room, each pair both twirling and circling. But only some of those that go counterclockwise are twirling counterclockwise. The others are twirling clockwise while circling counterclockwise. The same is true of those that are dancing around clockwise: some twirl clockwise, others twirl counterclockwise."

The twirling of waltzing couples proved an inspiration for Maria.

Lillian Gilbreth

Name: Lillian Moller Gilbreth
Born: 1868, Oakland, California
Died: 1972, Phoenix, Arizona
Occupation: Industrial engineer, psychologist
Education: University of California, Brown University
Major discoveries and achievements: Improving efficiency in the workplace and the home through time and motion studies
Major honors: First honorary member of the Society of Women Engineers, awarded the Hoover Medal of the American Society of Civil Engineers, 1966

The young Lillian Moller studied hard and did well at high school. At this time, women were not encouraged to pursue further education, and in order to continue her studies, she told her father that she could help out at home while also studying. Her first degree was in English literature, because as a woman it was hard to find anywhere that would allow her to study for a degree in science. It was not until 1915 that she gained her PhD in psychology from Brown University.

In 1904, Lillian married industrial engineer Frank Gilbreth. Frank was interested in trying to make the work of bricklayers more efficient, and Lillian found this study fascinating. She and Frank developed ways of analyzing the methods that bricklayers used. They looked at how they positioned their bodies, and at what point they became tired during the day. Lillian's psychology training added a new dimension to these studies. She was able to describe how people acted because of how they felt.

Lillian Gilbreth brought up 12 children. In 1948, two of them wrote a book about their unconventional upbringing. *Cheaper by the Dozen* was also made into a movie.

The Gilbreths tried to help workers to make the best use of their time. Some workers, however, were opposed to their ideas. They said it would mean more work for the same pay.

Following the principle of atomic physics, which studies the basic particles that make up an atom, and how those small particles all fit together to make matter, the Gilbreths studied the interaction of a team of bricklayers. The Gilbreths were able to reduce the number of actions in bricklaying from 18 to 5. Bricklayers could now lay 350 bricks an hour instead of 120. After this success, Lillian and Frank formed Gilbreth Inc., to improve working practices in other companies. Their advertising slogan was "The One Best Way to Do Work." When Frank died in 1924, Lillian took charge of the business.

Lillian also applied her ideas to the home. She interviewed more than 4,000 women to figure out the best height for sinks, and other kitchen equipment. She invented the foot-pedal trash can and shelves in fridge doors. She also lectured on scientific management and was called "a genius in the art of living."

TIME AND MOTION

In the early 1900s, U.S. industry was trying to find ways to make itself more efficient. The mechanical engineer Frederick Taylor believed that by timing the working practices of employees, their efficiency could be improved. He thought that workers should be forced to work in the most efficient way, and to think as little as possible about what they were doing. His approach was criticized by the Gilbreths. They believed that more attention should be paid to the actual processes involved in performing a task, so that motion should be studied, not merely the time it took. They also believed that productivity in the long run would be better if workers were happy and interested in their work. The combination of Taylor's ideas with those of the Gilbreths led to the idea of "time and motion" as the basis for improving worker productivity and efficiency.

Hedy Lamarr

Name: Hedy Lamarr
Born: 1914, Vienna, Austria
Died: 2000, Casselberry, Florida
Occupation: Actor and physicist
Education: Self-taught in physics
Major discoveries and achievements: Improved radio-guidance system for torpedoes by changing radio frequencies
Major honors: Electronic Frontier Foundation's Pioneer Award, 1997

Hedwig Eva Maria Kiesler had twin interests as a teenager. One was acting, the other was inventing things. She won a beauty pageant at the age of just 12, and her acting career was launched soon after. After appearing in her first film in 1933, she married a wealthy Austrian weapons dealer, but she dreamed of Hollywood. In 1938, Kiesler's marriage ended. She moved to Hollywood, signed a contract with Louis B. Mayer, head of MGM pictures, and changed her name to Hedy Lamarr. Her screen career lasted from 1938 until the 1960s.

As well as being a successful actress, Hedy kept up her hobby as an inventor. As a teenager, she had worked on various inventions, including a traffic stoplight and a carbonated drink. In Hollywood, she had her own workshop where she experimented with ideas. She made suggestions about aviation design to the millionaire Howard Hughes. He allowed her to talk to the scientists and engineers that he employed on his private team.

Hedy's early inventions had not been successful. She said a carbonated drink that she devised "tasted like Alka Seltzer."

When World War II broke out, Hedy wanted to help. The U.S. Navy's advanced torpedoes were guided to their targets by radio signals. Radio signals, however, were easily jammed by the enemy, sending the torpedoes off course. Together with the music composer George Antheil, Hedy invented a system that changed the **frequency** of radio signals using a pattern that was only known to the ship's commander. The invention was granted a patent in 1942.

Hedy wanted to give up acting and move to the east coast to work as part of the National Inventors Council on war-related technology. However, she was persuaded that her fame as an actor could be more useful for raising money for military operations.

Hedy and Antheil's invention had a huge influence on the development of later technology. A version of it is used in Wi-Fi, barcode scanners, digital cellphones, email, and Bluetooth devices.

Although Hedy had success in Cecil B. DeMille's 1949 film *Samson and Delilah*, she always found inventing more interesting than acting.

CHANGING ARRANGEMENTS

When Hedy met her Hollywood neighbor, musician George Antheil, she realized that writing music for player pianos was a method that could also be used to create radio frequencies that jumped around. Player pianos play mechanically according to preset instructions. Antheil had once written a piece that used 16 player pianos. Lamarr and Antheil's patent used 88 frequencies, which was the same number as the keys on a standard keyboard. The keys were activated by a code on a punched paper tape. Hedy and George used the same method for programming radio signals for torpedoes. The changing pattern of 88 radio frequencies was impossible for an enemy to scan and jam before the torpedo had hit its target.

The piano "roll" on a player piano indicates which keys are to be played.

Donna Strickland

Name: Donna Strickland
Born: 1959, Guelph, Ontario, Canada
Occupation: Mathematician, electrical engineer, and astronomer
Education: McMaster University and University of Rochester
Major discoveries and achievements: Development of short-pulse, intense laser systems
Major honours: Nobel Prize in Physics, 2018

Donna Strickland's mother was a teacher and her father was an electrical engineer. They encouraged her science studies. Donna became fascinated by lasers after visiting the Toronto Science Center when she was just five years old. She loved physics and enjoyed her early student work studying engineering physics at McMaster University in Ontario. She studied for her PhD at the University of Rochester, where she was a researcher at the Laboratory for Laser Energetics.

Lasers produce a powerful beam of light that can be directed very precisely. It can cut through metal more accurately than a saw. Lasers are also used in medicine.

Microwave **radiation** is invisible, but in 1958, U.S. physicists Charles H. Townes and Arthur Schawlow proposed that it was possible to make a device that would give off visible light. The term "laser" stands for light amplification by stimulated emission of radiation. Another U.S. physicist, Theodore H. Maiman, finally made the first laser in 1960. Since then, lasers have been used in everything from major industry to making computer printers and compact discs to performing delicate eye surgery.

In 1997, Donna set up the "ultrafast laser group" at her laboratory at the University of Waterloo.

Donna's work as a research student involved trying to find a way of making lasers more effective. She worked with French scientist Gérard Mourou. Their aim was to increase the power of a laser beam. They achieved this by stretching out the laser, **amplifying** the pulse of the light beam, then compressing it again. This produced ultra-fast, ultra-sharp, and ultra-powerful laser beams. The results of the experiment, known as chirped pulse amplification (CPA), were published in 1985.

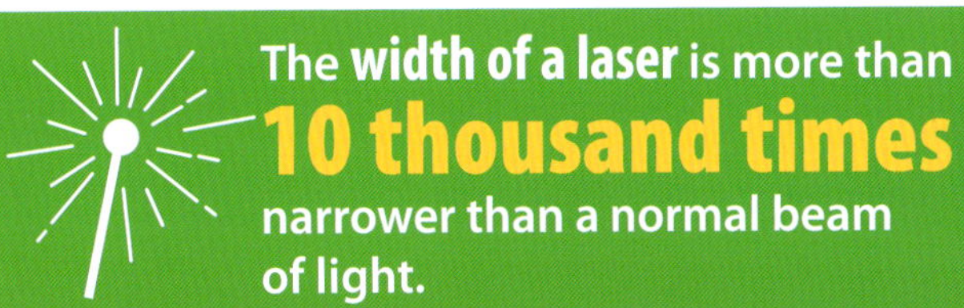

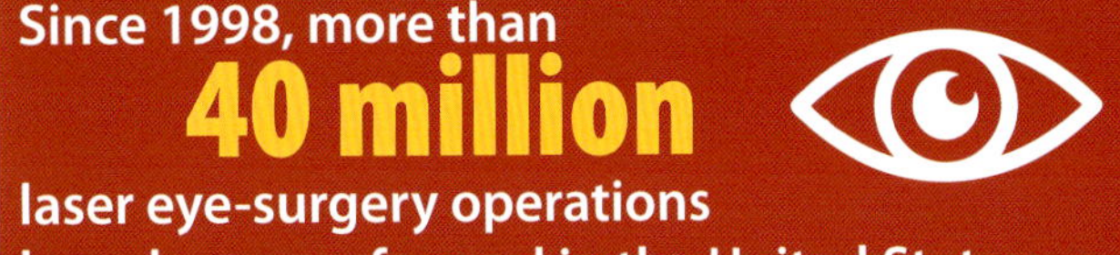

Chirped pulse amplification is used to make extremely precise cuts. It can cut through any substance and is so fast that it can even be used to study what happens inside atoms. Since its discovery, laser eye surgery has become possible and has benefitted millions of people worldwide. In 2018, Donna and Mourou shared the Nobel Prize in Physics for their discovery of CPA.

Timeline of Physics

Since the late nineteenth century, women have played a major role in the development of the science of physics. Many had to fight against tradition and prejudice to gain recognition. Science education was not open to most women. Today, many girls and women have equal opportunities to study physics alongside men. Teams of women and men are making groundbreaking advances in physics all over the globe.

1720 | 1800 | 1850 | 1900 | 1930

1732
Laura Bassi receives a PhD in physics from the Bologna University in Italy.

1826
Mary Somerville publishes her paper on her theories behind "The magnetic properties of the violet rays of the solar spectrum."

1906
Hertha Ayrton is awarded the prestigious Hughes Medal by the British Royal Society.

1939
Lise Meitner discovers nuclear fission.

Chien-Shiung Wu was one of the many women who worked on the atomic bomb. She joined the U.S. Manhattan Project in 1944, where she identified a problem that was causing a nuclear reactor to shut down.

1940 | 1970 | 1990 | 2000 | 2018

1941
Lillian Gilbreth becomes head of the Newark College of Engineering.

1963
Maria Goeppert Mayer wins the Nobel Prize for her work on the nuclear shell model of atomic structure.

1990s
Cynthia Breazeal invents the first "social robot." This robot learns from interaction with humans.

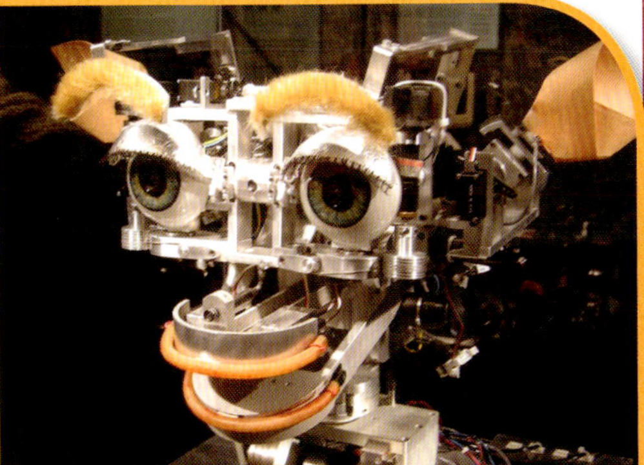

2014
Hedy Lamarr is admitted into the National Inventors Hall of Fame.

2018
Donna Strickland is awarded the Nobel Prize in Physics for her work on lasers.

Quiz

1 What Greek thinker proposed that all matter is composed of small atoms that we cannot see?

2 What was the gas that Hertha Ayrton found to be the cause of electric streetlights hissing?

3 What political movement did Hertha Ayrton support?

4 Lisa Meitner provided the theory behind what powerful force?

5 Why did Lisa Meitner have to leave Germany?

6 Lillian Gilbreth was famous for her practical inventions. What was the subject of her first degree?

7 For what did Maria Goeppert Mayer receive the Nobel Prize?

8 Why did Hedy Lamarr's frequency-hopping device have 88 frequencies?

9 What does "laser" stand for?

10 What is the main medical application of Donna Strickland's chirped pulse amplification?

ANSWERS

1. Democritus **2.** Oxygen **3.** Votes for women, the suffragette movement **4.** Nuclear fission **5.** Because she was Jewish **6.** Psychology **7.** For the nuclear shell model of atomic structure **8.** Because there are 88 keys on a standard piano keyboard **9.** Light amplification by stimulated emission of radiation **10.** Laser eye surgery

Key Words

Age of Enlightenment, The: a movement that began in Europe in the 1700s and spread throughout the world. It rejected the power of royal rulers and religious leaders in favor of logical thinking and science.

amplifying: in physics, the process of enlarging or increasing the oscillations of an electrical signal or light beam

atomic bomb: a bomb in which the explosive power is caused by the release of energy from splitting atoms, also called a nuclear bomb

atoms: tiny particles that are the basic units of matter

electromagnetism: a branch of physics that involves the study of how electric currents behave

frequency: a measurement of the number of times a sound wave vibrates in a period of time

gravity: a force that pulls two objects toward each other

matter: substance that everything physical is made from

nuclear fission: splitting an atom's nucleus to release a huge amount of energy

nucleus: the center part of an atom that consists of protons and neutrons

oxidation: reacting with oxygen

patented: to obtain the exclusive rights to an invention or process

philosopher: a person who thinks deeply and seriously about the meaning of life and the universe

radiation: electromagnetic energy, or visible light, is a form of radiation

Index

LIGHTBOX

SUPPLEMENTARY RESOURCES

Click on the plus icon found in the bottom left corner of each spread to open additional teacher resources.

- Download and print the book's quizzes and activities
- Access curriculum correlations
- Explore additional web applications that enhance the Lightbox experience

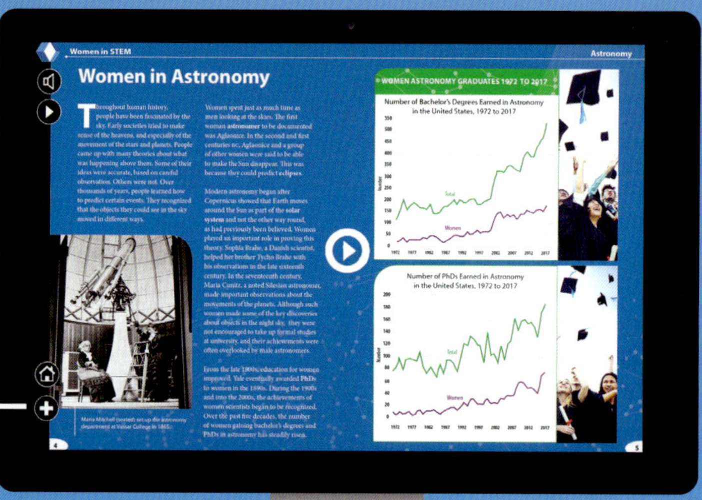

LIGHTBOX DIGITAL TITLES
Packed full of integrated media

VIDEOS

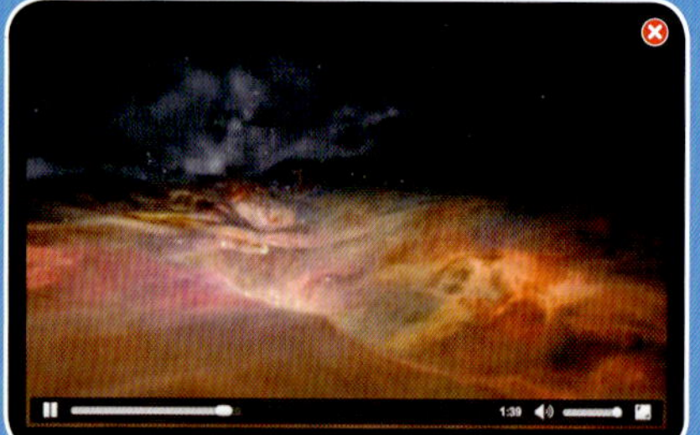

INTERACTIVE MAPS

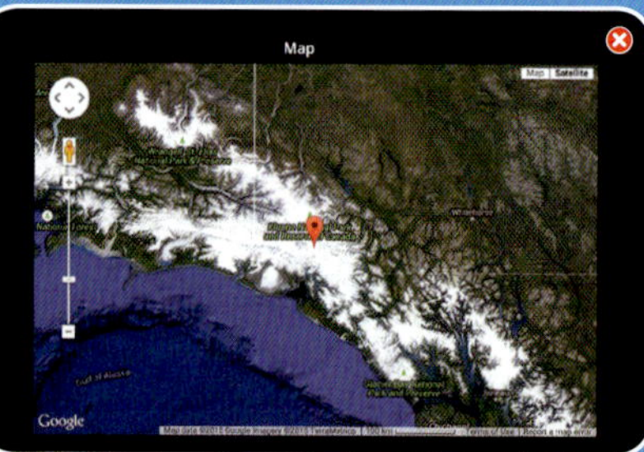

WEBLINKS

SLIDESHOWS

QUIZZES

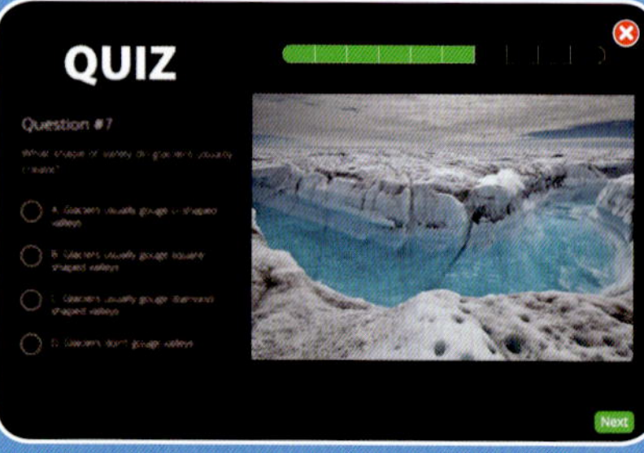

OPTIMIZED FOR

- ✓ TABLETS
- ✓ WHITEBOARDS
- ✓ COMPUTERS
- ✓ AND MUCH MORE!

Published by Smartbook Media Inc.
350 5th Avenue, 59th Floor New York, NY 10118
Website: www.openlightbox.com

Project Coordinator: Heather Kissock
Art Director: Terry Paulhus

Library of Congress Control Number: 2019941823

ISBN 978-1-5105-4437-6 (hardcover)
ISBN 978-1-5105-4438-3 (multi-user eBook)

Printed in Guangzhou, China
1 2 3 4 5 6 7 8 9 0 23 22 21 20 19

072019
311218

Photo Credits

Every reasonable effort has been made to trace ownership and to obtain permission to reprint copyright material. The publisher would be pleased to have any errors or omissions brought to its attention so that they may be corrected in subsequent printings.

The publisher acknowledges Getty Images, Alamy, and Shutterstock as its primary image suppliers for this title.